I0132622

This book is a work of fiction. Names,
characters, places and incidents are
products of the author's imagination or
are used fictitiously. Any resemblance to
actual events or locales or persons,
living or dead, is entirely coincidental.

Copyright© 2010 by Nicole Plain

All rights reserved, including the right
to reproduce this book or portions
thereof in any form whatsoever. For
information contact Your Time Publishing.

ISBN 098442332X
EAN-13 9780984423323
LCCN 2010938084

Reflections
of a
Life Lived

Poems by

Nicole Plain

Your Time Publishing, LLC P.O. Box 872365
New Orleans, Louisiana, 70187

Nicole Plain

Reflections
of a Life Lived

A special thanks to:

My mother for always being there and encouraging me,
my husband for opening my eyes to something better,
and to my kids for teaching me about unconditional
love. Lastly I would like to thank the rest of my family; I
am blessed to have all of them in my life. They have
always supported, loved and believed in me.

In Memory of
My Father

Your Time Publishing, LLC P.O. Box 872365
New Orleans, Louisiana, 70187

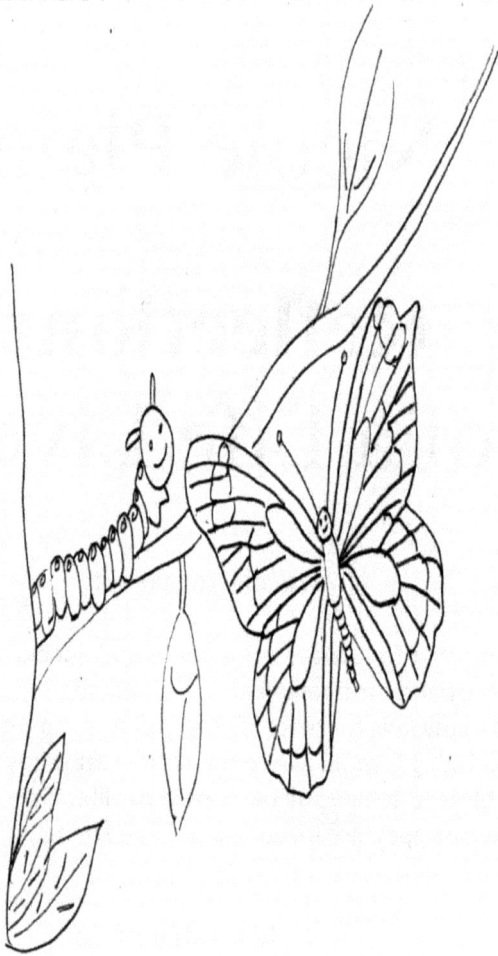

Like the caterpillar we all metamorphoses into the beautiful butterfly.

Nicole Plain, born and raised in New Orleans, Louisiana, Graduated from UNO 2003 BA Management and 2005 BA Accounting after a semester at the University of Texas, Arlington. She has now relocated to the Dallas area of Texas, but still loves her Saints. The love of writing has always been her release and any time she shared her writings with others they would comment on the quality and emotions that they invoked. This is her first publication and if we are blessed this won't be her last.

Table of Content

Reflections of a Life Lived

NP

My Perfect Man,

If I could build a man from scratch,

What would I first request,

That he be 5'11, chocolate and handsome of course,

A hard worker that knows what he wants,
a God-fearing man

A man that would always lend a helping hand

A little stubborn, so that no one could push him
around

But strong so that he wouldn't let anything bring
him down,

Faithful and loyal and true to his family

Intelligent but some how not come across as
arrogant

NP

He doesn't always like to admit when he has made a mistake

But man enough to step up and take whatever comes his way

A man that can still smile at his wife,

Even when she is complaining and fussing about her life.

A man who knows me better than I know myself

And loves me unconditionally despite my faults

My perfect man isn't A Perfect Man you see,

He is just the Perfect Man for me.

NP

My Wedding Day

Today is my Wedding Day,

A day every woman dreams of in some kind of way,

I check my hair and make-up as I put on my dress,

I have done everything possible to look my best,

My family and close friends have come to celebrate with me,

I am nervous as ever, hoping that my future husband will love what he sees,

As I walk down the aisle, I can see him smile

And at that moment I know that it is real,

The love that we both share and feel.

I reach out to grab his hand, so that we can stand

NP

And take a vow as husband and wife,

To be there for one another for the rest of our life.

As the reverend says you may now kiss your bride,

I turn to my husband and look him straight in the eye,

And we kiss for the first time

And I know in my heart that he is mine.

NP

Delivery

When you get that sharp pain in your side,

Sometimes making you feel as if you are going to die,

And then the pain intensifies,

And you are lying there with tears in your eyes,

You are begging anyone and everyone for help

And then you start to blame yourself,

Wondering if this feeling is really worth it

Then you start to panic,

Because the pains are coming with every breath

And you think to yourself that this is nothing like you expect, you beg everyone for some kind of relief

NP

Hoping that someone will feel your grief

And then you are told to please be still

*As they stick you with a device that looks like a
sharp long nail*

The pain slowly begins to die down

As the warm feeling starts to move around

Someone now tells you that you can begin to push

And you want to tell everyone in the room to hush,

*So now you are pushing for what feels like
eternity,*

*And out comes a head, and you start to feel your
destiny.*

You push again, hoping that this will be the end

NP

As you feel something leaving your body,

you know it is a Godsend

Is it okay, was it able to find its way.

Then there is a pause and you start to hear a little noise

As the doctor hands you your little bundle of joy.

Congratulations it's a boy......

NP

Happy Mother's Day

To a mother that has been there every step of the
way,

That supports you in everything you say,

A mother that has cried with you through the
toughest days,

Who has felt your pain, even when you hadn't
explained and pushed her away.

Who sticks by your side whether you are right or
wrong,

Who is always there with a cheerful song,

Who can laugh with you through the happiest of
times,

Who will not judge you because of that special
bond

A mother who isn't ashamed to stand by you,

NP

Even sometimes when you have been a fool,

Someone who forgives you again and again,

Someone who is not only a mother but a friend,

Someone who has given you all of what she has,

And all she asks in return is for you to do your best.

A mother that makes you feel like you are on top of the world,

And who has loved you unconditionally since you were a little girl,

I would like to say to the special mother in my life,

Happy Mother's Day, mom and yes you were always right.....

NP

NP

Growing Up

He is no longer my baby anymore

It frightens me every time he walks out the door
I don't want to let him go

But I know he needs his space in order to grow

I have to trust that I have raised him right

And I can't always keep him in my sight.

For parents, this is probably the hardest day

When you realize your child has to go his own way

And discover all the things that we have already done

And have tried to protect and shield them from

I know in my heart that I have to give him a chance to explore

NP

Because I know he will spread his wings and soar

Yet still I sit here afraid,

Knowing that the bumps ahead of him will be grave

But I know that I have to be brave

And trust that my little boy will always be safe....

NP

Adulthood

*Once you become a teenager, you can't wait to
become an adult,*

*You think to yourself that this will be the best
result,*

When no one can no longer tell you what to do,

*You sit back and wonder and say man this is going
to be cool.*

*So you wait and wait for the day that couldn't be
seen,*

And the day finally comes when you turn eighteen,

*You think to yourself that your parents will no
longer be the boss of you,*

*And from now until forever you can do what you
want to do.*

NP

But after a few dropped classes and expired bus passes,

You realize that you aren't all that grown up at all,

And will be moving back home by the end of the fall,

So then you think back to that feeling you had when you thought you were grown,

And you say to yourself, man I am so glad to be back home.......

Adulthood comes with time, not with an age

So take your time and figure it out

before rushing to that next stage.

NP

Graduation Day

Congratulations, today is your graduation,

A time when family stops by to pay their regards

Because all your hard work has finally paid off.

*No more studying and cramming all night, this is
surely a delight.*

It is time to put on your cap and gown,

And lead the way to a familiar sound.

*As you pass your family by, you can see the look in
their eyes.*

That they are proud as they cheer your name,

*You wonder what could I have done to gain such
fame.*

*As you wait for your name to be called you can
barely sit still,*

NP

notation*

Sitting there wondering how good it will feel

When you are handed your certificate to
acknowledge your new found skill.

It is time to stand now to get your recognition,

And you think to yourself that you are almost
finish this long Expedition.

You smile for the camera as you accept your
certificate

Anticipating that this will be a great benefit

When you are done you walk back to your seat

Knowing that your journey is now complete.

NP

Wake Up

Your relationship has come to an end.

But you pretend you want to stay friends.

As soon as he doesn't answer your call,

You begin to act crazy and say things off the wall

You say you wish he was dead, and your face
starts to turn all red,

But you say you are glad that it is over,

But since the break up you haven't been sober.

Doing any and everything to get his attention,

But then you turn around and wish he was in
prison,

Why would a person wish such devious things on
another,

NP

Do you not realize that he is my brother.

You need to wake up, and move on

Give your heart a chance to mourn.

You are filled with so much hate and anger

Sometimes I get scared that you may put yourself in danger.

These feelings you have are not healthy

I wish you could just wake up and see,

You two just weren't meant to be.

NP

Stressed

Stress comes in all shapes and sizes

And if you decide not to deal with it, it somehow monopolizes,

It starts with headaches and chest aches that can not be explained

Doctors start to look and treat you as if you are going insane

It takes away your happiness

And makes you feel uneasy and restless

Stress has killed a lot of people in some unexplained deaths,

And that's because it consumes you and leave both you and your body inept

For those of you who don't know it, don't underestimate stress

NP

*It can take away loved ones and jobs and leave you
with a lot less.*

Stress attacks your heart, mind and soul

And leaves you with an empty hole

That can never be refilled or regained

And it keeps you in constant pain.

We all face stress in some form or fashion

*So don't ignore it, or all of this is bound to
happen......*

NP

Control

Why do you let him control your life?

Isn't it obvious that his intentions aren't right?

You don't even put up a fight,

It is either his way or the highway,

And you are so afraid of losing him that you put your feelings aside,

Hoping that will make him happy and keep him satisfied.

But every time you give in to him, you lose a part of yourself.

He will take and take until there is nothing left.

Making you feel more and more empty, broken and scorned

Your heart will be torn,

NP

And of course he won't want you then because
your mind and body will be all worn

But unfortunately this is something you can not
predict,

In your mind you will always be his.

Just as long as you continue to let him have his
way,

You think eventually you will be rewarded with
your wedding day.

But the truth is whether he decides to say I do

He will repeatedly continue to

Keep Control over you....

NP

Settling

Why is it that we settle?

You have been in a relationship for longer than 5 years,

And your guy keeps saying that marriage is what he fears,

So instead of moving on, you figure you are being wrong.

So you stay and wait a little longer.

Another year passes by

And you are still wondering why

So you bring it up again in hopes that this will be the end

And that he will finally say yes, but of course you fail that test

NP

Because he still isn't ready

So you tell yourself hold steady

And that he is the one

Because your lives together have already begun,

Why is it that we settle?

Now 5 years have turned into 10

And you are wondering why you are still living in sin

So you go to your guy in hopes that he will see the light

But this time all he says is goodnight.

NP

A True Friend

There aren't many of us, who get to have a true
friend,

Someone who will be there for you until the end.

The person you tell all your secrets to because you
know they will not judge you,

The first person you call when you are feeling blue,

A person who you can laugh with about the silliest
of things,

And one you can also cry with because of the
hardships this world brings.

A true friend will be there on your wedding day,

And when the death of a loved one comes along,

They will sit with you even when there is nothing
to say.

NP

A true friend is someone who always understands,

And when they know you are coming to town they always change their plans.

Just so they can see you and give you a hug,

And treat you as if you have the same blood.

Of all the friends you meet, only 1 or 2 will be true

And I am happy to say that one of them is you.

NP

My Dearest friend

I once had a friend many years ago,

She was the kind of friend everyone would like to know.
She was kind and giving and enjoyed living.

We were teenagers back then,

Taking for granted where our lives were going and not being cautious of where we'd been.

My dearest friend became a single mother at the age of fifteen,

Disappointing her family because this was surely unforeseen.

A few years went by and my friend and I were separated by our different lives.

But we would keep in touch from time to time

Just to let each other know that we were still fine.

NP

One day my friend called and asked me to take a seat,

She said she had been infected with HIV

And I wondered how could this be,

Since we were only in our early twenties.

She said apparently she had been living with it for some time now

Because unfortunately that wasn't the only thing the doctor's found.

She said she had several different STD's,

And of course at this time I just dropped to my knees.

I asked my friend why wasn't she taking care of her body,

She said she trusted the guy and didn't think

NP

he had anything to hide.

She said lately she had thoughts of suicide

And had been admitted to the hospital for trying to end her life.

Her mother died not many months after that

I believe the facts were just too much for her to accept.

And my friend blamed herself for her mother's death.

Not even a year later I heard the worst news,

My friend's body was discovered by search and rescue

They said she drowned after a hurricane came through

NP

*But I believe my friend had just given up on her
will to survive,*

And just decided it would be easier to die.

Thoughts of my friend still haunt me to this day

*I wish I could have been there more for her and
offered more to say.*

*But instead I am here mourning my friend wishing
she had chosen another way.*

NP

Grandparents

Only the most fortunate of kids get to have living
grandparents in their lives

And if you are very lucky you will have some on
both sides.

Someone to watch over you and give you
everything your heart desires,

Someone you will always admire.

A lot like parents but don't need to show
authority,

And every time you are with them it is like a great
big party.

They will usually cook your favorite foods,

And travel a thousand miles just to see you.

They always show up with some kind of treat or
treasure,

NP

That they know will be a great pleasure.

*They sometimes will fuss with your parents for you
to have your way*

*And you think to yourself that this must be my
lucky day.*

*They are a lot like parents but definitely more
majestic*

*And if you had your way they are exactly what
you would have selected*

Now we know why they are called Grand

*They will always love and spoil you, because that
was God's plan.*

NP

The Mother-n-law

Have you ever had a mother-n-law who couldn't
stand your guts?

One who never really got to know you because her
mind was already made up.

A mother-n-law who thought her son would put
her first,

But of course she was wrong and that bubble was
burst.

A woman who wants to see the bad in you just to
prove she was right,

And because of that all everyone can do is fight.

Someone who calls her son over and over with
negative thoughts about you,

That makes you uncomfortable when you here them
talking so you have to leave the room.

NP

She always manages to upset you and ruin your
day,

But then pretends to be naïve and set in her ways.

A woman who has managed to bring you and your
man closer together,

Because in the end she makes him realize his family
is what is forever.

But his mother can't accept that and so she
disapproves

And for that her and her son's relationship will
forever be doomed.

NP

What about the Children

I sit in silence every day, wondering about the
Children of today.

Our young mothers are not focusing on our
children's needs,

And for that our kids are suffering indeed.

No one is there to love them and show them the
way, and offer positive things to say.

So they grow up uneducated, uncaring and
irresponsible.

And soon find themselves in some kind of obstacle.

But all of this could have been prevented,

And one less child could have not been
apprehended,

If our parents would have just taken more time,

NP

To be there for our kids and help them to shine.

It doesn't take much to please a child and help them to be successful,

All you have to do is show them love that is unconditional.

But instead our parents are doing the opposite

And leaving our poor kids to be unfit.

They are not being given what they need to survive.

And it is only a matter of time before they ruin their lives

Our children's future is at stake

And it depends on the choices that we make.

And so the question still stands,

NP

"*What about the children of today*",

Will anyone ever stand up and help them to not go astray.

NP

NP

Will the real Father please stand up?

You call yourself a dad, and if you believe that you
are truly sad.

You don't even know your own child, are you
living in some kind of denial.

How do you even sleep at night?

Do you ever wake up in a fright?

Wondering if your child is even safe,

Can you even remember his face?

His birthday has passed many years, and the idea

that you don't even call should bring tears.

But I would like you to know that he doesn't even
get mad,

Because in his mind you are not his real dad.

NP

You are just the man that contributed to his creation,

And for that it is truly a celebration.

But to us that is all we can say thank you for,

For your sake, I really wish we could say more,

But unfortunately you will live with the regret of never knowing your first born

And for that your heart will forever mourn.

NP

I Love you, I Hate you

I love you, I hate you, I love you, I hate you

Some days are great and I feel like you are my soul mate,

And other days are bad when you make me feel so sad,

We have been playing this game for several years now

And I feel as though we are just going round and round

I want to love you every day but how can I when you make me feel this way,

I want commitment and you want to be free

But when I say I am going to leave then it is all about me.

NP

When the bad outweighs the good,

and I have done everything that I could

I will walk away and you will not be able to make me stay

The days are getting harder to bear

And I can't think of one reason to still care.

There is no longer a force that binds us together,

I love you and I hate you but I think this is the end of our forever.

NP

Taking Lives

Why is it that people kill?

Is it because they can not feel.

How can you choose to end someone's life?

Is it because it makes them feel alive,

They take away mothers, fathers, sisters, brothers, sons, and daughters,

Is it because of their own childhood horrors?

They treat murder as if it is a game,

Is it because they are insane.

They like to pick the gullible and innocent,

Is it because they are too naïve to know their true intent.

NP

*But sometimes they take the strong and
sophisticated,*

Is it because they fear where their lives are fated.

Why is it that people kill?

*Is it because we as a people are meant to suffer,
regardless of our race or color.*

*Or is it just something that we will never
comprehend,*

That will continue to go on again and again,

*And we will forever wonder about until we reach
our end.*

NP

His story

When he met her, it was love at first sight.

And not even two years later all they do is fight.

She is ready to take their relationship to the next stage,

He feels as though he is trapped in a cage.

He decides he doesn't want the commitment,

And he has to tell her so that there will be no resentment.

So he leaves this young lady,

But of course to find out now that there is a baby.

Now he feels it is time to take some responsibility,

And show his ex-lady he now has the ability,

To settle down and raise a family.

NP

But it is too late; her heart is now filled with so much hate.

She still can't get pass him leaving her

And for that she feels that he must suffer.

So a baby is born, and a family is torn

Because no one can stop and ask for forgiveness.

So he now moves on, in hopes of finding someone

That he can build a life with

So he carefully waits for someone he sees fit,

But he makes yet another bad pick,

When he finds out he has slipped

And will be the father of yet one more daughter.

NP

He knows he isn't ready for one more kid,

But he knows he too could have prevented this

So this time he sticks by his lady

And welcomes into the world yet another baby.

But still he wonders about his first born

And can't help but to mourn,

He still waits for the day

When he can be reunited with his baby

And can be a proud father

Of not one but both of his daughters...

NP

Faith

How strong is your faith?

Is it something you hold sacred?

Does it change with every situation?

Or do you hold on with no hesitation.

Is it easier to have faith when things go your way?

And then you lose sight when your life is in
dismay.

Do you place the blame on others?

Or do you trust what the Lord has for you to
discover.

How strong is your faith?

Is it something you rely on day after day?

NP

Or do you question it in every single way?

When the most unimaginable has happened in your

life do you still have faith?

*Or do you curse God because at this point your
heart is filled with so much hate?*

How strong is your faith?

NP

Uncle

Today we celebrate the death of a loved one,
he was my grandmother's only son,

We shouldn't be sad, because he will soon be
joining his dad,

Where he will be reunited with his maker,

Who is known to all of us as our Savior,
we need to rejoice,

And know that this was God's choice,

He is in a better place now, so why should we
frown, we know that we will see him again,

This is definitely not the end.

But still we sit here in mourning,

Knowing that this death is some type of warning,

NP

That our lives on this place will eventually come to
an end,

And our everlasting lives will soon begin,

And all will be left here is the family we left
behind,

I think that is the hardest part about dying.

But we have to be strong, and know that this isn't
wrong.

We must accept the fact that his life here is
complete,

And that another chance will come when we will
meet,

But for now we have to continue to live and
strive,

And keep the memory of our loved one alive.

NP

May 1st

Today is the day that my father was born,
but right now I sit here torn.

Wondering if today should be a day of celebration,
or just a day of meditation,

Where I sit in silence and wonder about my father,

And think about whether he should have fought
harder,

To be there for his son and daughter.

But all of these are thoughts that can never be put
to rest,

Because my father decided to do what he thought
was best,

Which was leave his children behind at the ages of
fourteen and nine.

NP

When we barely knew or understood anything
about dying.

Today he would have turned fifty two,

And his life would have been filled with so many
blessings he wouldn't have known what to do.

But instead he focused on that one bad day,

And he just didn't see any other way.

So today I sit here on my father's birthday,

Wishing he would have considered what we would
have had to say.

NP

You Chose Death

Why did you choose death?

Did you change your mind before that last breath?

There were people here that loved and needed you,

Now what are we supposed to do.

The days have turned into years,

And the thought of you still brings tears,

Was it the fear, or did you just know that your end
was near.

There are so many questions that were left
unanswered,

A family left behind, was that even considered

So many promises that weren't kept,

NP

This is still so hard for me to accept.

I have heard if you take your life you can not be forgiven,

So does that mean I won't see you in heaven?

I pray everyday, in hopes that you will be spared

But then I wonder why should I even care.

The truth is that I love and miss you

I still wonder today if you even knew.

Is that why you chose Death,

But I still wonder if you knew right before you took your last breath.

NP

I Forgive You

*I have been carrying around this guilt and pain for
far too long,*

We both know that what you did was wrong,

*You have always treated me and my family as if
we weren't good enough*

*And because of that I have allowed my heart to fill
with disgust*

*But now the time has come to put an end to all of
this stuff*

*And move forward and closer to God because in
Him I trust.*

So today I say I forgive you with all of my heart.

And hopefully this will lead us to a better start.

NP

Forgive Me

Why is it so hard to forgive,

Is it because we are afraid to relive,

What someone has said or done to us,

And we would rather not make a fuss.

Or is it because of the pain that they have caused,

Or maybe because we can now see their flaws,

None of us are perfect and we all make mistakes,

So forgive me now so that we can become closer to

God in Faith.

NP

A Mother Scorned

When I was a little girl my mother once asked me what I wanted to be when I grew up,

My answer was to be a mother,

I thought God created us to do no other.

I remember her giving me a look as if I had so much more to discover.

I was married in the summer of 1980,

And by thanksgiving would be expecting my first baby.

She was everything I dreamed of in a child

But my husband on the other hand was still a bit wild.

He wanted to party and drank and hang out until dawn,

But all I ever wanted was for us to be with our first born.

NP

*So there began the separation that would last for
15 years*

*Only if I would have known that he would bring
me so many tears.*

*So the years went by as me and my husband
lived our double lives,*

*Where we would appear to be the perfect family
to all who cared*

*And would fuss and fight at home because he
never was there.*

*The late nights and fights continued for what
seemed like eternity,*

*And then I prayed and asked the Lord to give me
the eyes to see.*

And there it was as clear as day, for

14 years my husband had his way.

NP

A Mother Scorned
(Cont.)

He had been cheating on me for all this time,

And here I thought he was only mine.

I knew I had to let him go, but how could I when
he had provided for so long.

So I stepped out on faith and filed for a divorce,

He had pretty much left me with no recourse.

So there I was with no home and practically
making minimum wage,

Thinking to myself this is not where I thought
I would be at this age.

My husband decided to act really funny and not
give me or the kids any money.

I prayed and trusted that the Lord would see us
through

NP

Because at this point I had no idea of what to do.

Then one day I got a phone call that my husband
had died.

I was sick to my stomach because he was only
thirty five.

What could have taken this healthy man's life,

Somebody please answer as I am his wife.

All I can remember is his brother saying it was the
bullet that killed him,

And then for a second my mind went blank, as I
tried to gather all of what he was saying.

Apparently my husband just didn't die but he
decided to end his life.

This was something I just couldn't comprehend,

And I wasn't sure how I was going to tell his
children.

NP

A Mother Scorned
(Cont.)

Two weeks before my birthday and I am at my
husband's funeral sitting on the front isle.

When I noticed this little girl's smile.

It looked quite familiar and scary at the same time.

Because then I realized that she looked exactly
like my daughter except she wasn't mine.

So there came my mother-n-law to break the news,

That my daughter and son had a sister that they
never knew.

She was one year older than my son and there was
nothing I could say or do.

So there I was broke, hurt, angry and afraid,

And hoping that God could show me the way.

NP

And he answered in the form of a check,

It was enough money to get me and my kids out of this wreck.

The first thing we did was bought a new place,

I can remember the excitement I could see in my kids faces.

There aren't many days where I don't think of my husband

and the question my mother asked me so long ago.

My answer would probably be the same except this time I know,

That being a mother is great but having someone

to share that with is the ultimate fate.........

NP

Needs vs Wants

Why do we as women feel that we need a man,

Someone to walk with us along the sand,

Who we feel will always lend a hand
,
And that he is the only one who can

Make us feel like a woman.

Ladies, do we really need a man?

Or do we just crave a man

Because that was God's plan,

And it has been this way since life began.

But do we really need a man?

To make us feel like a woman,

To take care of us even though we can,

NP

To walk with us and hold our hand.

Even though we are not children.

Do we as strong, independent women really need a man????????

NP

www.ingramcontent.com/pod-product-compliance
Lightning Source LLC
Chambersburg PA
CBHW071020040426
42443CB00007B/877